# GOLF

## How to Look Good When You're Not

### GEOFF HOWSON

**CB**

CONTEMPORARY
BOOKS

CHICAGO · NEW YORK

**Library of Congress Cataloging-in-Publication Data**

Howson, George F.
  Golf : how to look good when you're not.

  1. Golf—Anecdotes, facetiae, satire, etc.   I. Title.
PN6231.G68H69     1988        796.352      87-37974
ISBN 0-8092-4659-7 (pbk.)

Published by Contemporary Books, Inc.
180 North Michigan Avenue, Chicago, Illinois 60601
Manufactured in the United States of America
Library of Congress Catalog Card Number: 87-37974
International Standard Book Number: 0-8092-4659-7

Published simultaneously in Canada by Beaverbooks, Ltd.
195 Allstate Parkway, Valleywood Business Park
Markham, Ontario L3R 4T8 Canada

As this endeavor drew to a close my thoughts—as they often do—drifted to my Dad. This one's for him. I think he would have laughed.

# CONTENTS

# I.

# BASICALLY GOLF

Ponder for a moment . . .
A Theorem:

On the average a maximum of 4.097 percent of
the time associated with a round of golf is
spent whacking the golf ball with a golf club.

A Proof:

Step 1.  Average time spent on
the golf course
(18 holes).................. 14,400 seconds

Average time spent on
pre- and postgame
social activities............+ 7,200 seconds

Total time associated
with a game............... 21,600 seconds

Step 2.  Worst reported score
(18 holes)...................     177 strokes

Average time spent per
stroke.......................    × 5 seconds*

Total time spent
whacking the ball........     885 seconds

Step 3.  Total time spent
whacking the ball........     885 seconds

Total time associated
with a game............... 21,600 seconds

3

Step 4.   Step 3 expressed as a
          percentage................  4.097 percent

It follows quite logically from our theorem and proof that if one spends a *maximum* of 4.097 percent of one's time on and around a golf course swinging a golf club at a golf ball, one must then be spending a *minimum* of 95.903 percent of one's time on and around a golf course doing something *other* than whacking that bloody little ball.

Now, if you happen to be one of the vast majority of people who have never before set foot on a golf course, you are probably wondering just what in blue blazes is going on out and about a golf course during this other 95.903 percent of the time.

Well, the fact of the matter is that all sorts of bloody things are going on out there, some of which are downright torturous and all of which are remarkably time-consuming.

A few moments of somewhat typical golf course antics are captured in the following illustration, and even the most casual observer will realize that during the entire 7-minute and 12-second time span, the act of striking a golf ball with a golf club occurred only once.

Most of the time was consumed by such activities as walking to the ball, consulting the caddy, and harassing the caddy, which represent but a very small sample of what has come to be called *non-golf-ball-striking activities.*

A description of some of the more common non-golf-ball-striking activities constitutes the bulk of this chapter, and one should bear in mind as one reviews this abridged listing that as diverse as these activities may appear to be, they all have one very important thing in common: *none of these activities actually involves striking a golf ball with a golf club!*

Now, it is a matter of fact that until your golfing compatriots actually see you hit that tiny little ball with the big old club they can only guess as to the caliber of your golf game.

A second matter of fact is that golfers are by nature a competitive lot, and as a result your golfing compatriots will be extremely curious as to the quality of your golf game.

If these curious and competitive fellows can't be privy to your actually taking a whack at the ball, on just what are they going to base their assumptions as to the quality of your game?

Of course! The little snoops are going to base their assumptions on what you're doing the 95.903 percent of the time you're *not* hitting a golf ball.

While a multitude of literature offering advice and instruction as to how to master the 4.097 percent of your game that involves striking the ball already exists, there has been virtually no literature dedicated to the mastering of the non-golf-ball-striking activities of the game.

Just as there is a right way and a wrong way to strike a golf ball, there is a right way and a wrong way to perform the many non-golf-ball-striking activities.

It is the purpose of this book, then, to offer instruction in the proper manner in which to behave, dress, and equip oneself such that one can easily master almost 96 percent of one's golf game.

I should mention at this juncture, however, that mastering the 4.097 percent of one's game that actually involves striking a golf ball is bloody well impossible, and the best advice to be offered from these pages is that you *never take up the game.*

# BALL MARKING

Contrary to the image conjured up by the name of this event, it does *not* involve making little marks on one's golf ball.

Ball marking instead refers to the odd little ritual of marking the position of one's golf ball on the putting green such that its presence will not interfere with another golfer's attempt to putt his golf ball into the hole.

Not unlike the greeting at a Japanese steak house, this activity involves much bowing and scurrying about and proves quite time-consuming over 18 holes of golf.

AT THE REQUEST OF HIS OPPONENT, OLAF MARKED THE
POSITION OF HIS BALL.

# BROWSING AND PURCHASING

In reality, browsing and purchasing are two distinct events, but they are so closely related as to be considered a single activity.

The true hub of this activity is the pro shop, where all manner of golf equipment and attire is on display at astronomical prices.

Absurd pricing notwithstanding, haggling over price in the confines of the pro shop is considered quite naughty and may well result in one's removal from the premises.

In contrast, however, browsing is not only permitted but encouraged within the confines of the pro shop and it takes place with a vengeance.

Surprisingly, browse time is abused more by men than by women because the golf course is one of the few areas where men are allowed to exercise their fashion sense—or, more precisely, their sense of humor!

THE GOLF COURSE IS ONE OF THE FEW PLACES WHERE A BUFFOON MIGHT COMFORTABLY DRESS THE PART.

# Caddy Harassment

Caddy harassment is a general heading for a wide variety of activities aimed at making life absolutely miserable for one's caddy. These activities usually begin shortly after the golfer's first pathetic attempt to swat a golf ball and increase in frequency and severity with the deterioration of the golfer's game.

While caddy harassment typically takes the form of high-pitched verbal abuse, more spectacular forms of abuse have developed over the years.

CADDY HARASSMENT: THE BALL BOB.

## *GRAPHITE CONDUCTIVITY TEST*

Introduced by one L. A. Hayes in 1977, this methodology stemmed from an argument over the hazards of investigating light sockets with wooden pencils.

Hayes vehemently argued that the graphite in a wooden pencil is a prime conductor of electricity; thus it proved unfortunate for the caddy that Mr. Hayes (a) was having a particularly bad day on the golf course and (b) noticed the approach of a thunderstorm.

Having shackled the caddy to a lone tree near the fairway, Mr. Hayes stuffed his graphite-shafted driver into the caddy's pants and retreated to the comforts of the clubhouse as the storm drew near.

Ironically, the argument was never resolved, because it couldn't be determined whether it was the graphite shaft or the steel manacles that attracted the lightning.

The test did, however, prove that bolts of lightning can have a dramatic and rather adverse effect on the life expectancy of a caddy.

THE GRAPHITE CONDUCTIVITY TEST

## SWAN DIVE

Seething over the fact that her caddy refused to retrieve her golf ball from a shallow pool of quicksand, Ms. Catrina D'Cajon initiated perhaps the most gratifying method of caddy harassment yet devised.

Several holes after the quicksand incident, the caddy and Ms. D'Cajon found themselves on an elevated tee overlooking a dried-up riverbed some 400 feet below.

Ms. D'Cajon sneaked up behind the caddy, who had inadvertently strayed to the edge of the bluff, and after wedging her 3-iron between the caddy's legs belted the caddy in the back of the head with her bumbershoot and into a rather spectacular tumbling exercise down the side of the bluff.

After miraculously surviving his trip to the riverbed below, the caddy, so as not to lose his tip, then found himself in the unenviable position of retrieving all the golf equipment that had been ejected from the golf bag during the descent!

# CHEATING

Inasmuch as an entire chapter of this book is dedicated to a detailed discussion of this activity, we will defer an analysis of cheating to Chapter 3 and instead consider some of the time-consuming side effects of this non-golf-ball-striking activity.

Cheating occurs both on and off the golf course with a frequency so high as to be difficult to comprehend. Thus it is totally incomprehensible that the frequency with which one is *caught* cheating is so low.

When an individual *is* caught cheating, a tedious ceremony, so familiar to golfers that one can recognize it as such from several holes away, occurs:

1. Accuser calmly brings to the attention of the cheater the fact that the cheater has just been caught cheating.
2. The cheater calmly informs the accuser that he (the accuser) is a lying sonuvabitch.
3. Accuser, angered by the denial, breaks into a markedly more audible rendition of the accusation, beginning with "Why you. . . ."
4. The cheater returns the volley.
5. Accuser and cheater go about the task of punching each other about the head and shoulders.

CHEATING: THE TRAP HOOK

# CHIT CHAT

The arguing mentioned under "Cheating" is but one category of verbal communication that falls under the general heading of *chitchat.*

Chitchat can be pleasant or unpleasant in nature, and many of the chitchat categories, such as gossip and talking shop, take place in the real world as well as on the golf course.

Most chitchat occurs in the midst of other activities, like driving a golf cart such that it does not consume additional non-golf-ball-striking time. Two categories of chitchat, however, consume a great deal of time because they are intentionally conducted at a time when other activities will not prove a distraction.

## HANDICAP HYPE

The term *handicap* refers to the number of strokes a golfer may *legally* deduct from his (usually) gross score to arrive at his net score, thus reflecting the quality of the golfer's game; i.e., the higher the handicap, the worse the golfer.

Golfers always lie about their handicaps! Off the course they will always understate their actual handicap for the sake of image, and on the course they will always overstate their handicap, particularly during "Name Your Poison."

HANDICAP HYPE: FANTWELL AND FARNSWORTH DISCUSS A SLIGHT DISCREPANCY IN FARNSWORTH'S REPORTED HANDICAP.

## *NAME YOUR POISON*

This discussion usually takes place on the first tee and refers to the conversation among golfers about to play a match as to what game and rules will be played and how much money will be wagered; e.g., $2 Nassau, $1 Skins Game, and so on.

# Club Selection

To a certain extent club selection involves the chitchat activity in that verbal communication takes place between one's partner and/or caddy over such matters as wind direction and velocity, distance of the shot, and the like.

Beyond the chitchat, a good number of other time-consuming antics are associated with this activity, such as throwing little clumps of dirt in the air to test for wind direction and crouching behind one's ball to inspect the line of flight to the green.

Invariably, the exercise proves a total waste of time, because after a 10-minute interlude of club selection one typically smacks the bloody ball out of bounds or into the nearest body of water.

Still, having a good club selection routine can do much to enhance one's image as a golfer.

CLUB SELECTION: THE CADDY CONSULTATION

# Divot Replacement

Divots are clods of earth and grass that are removed from the natural terrain when one's club comes into contact with the ground during a swing.

Obviously, the number of divots to be replaced depends on the number of swings a golfer takes, such that a poor golfer might spend a remarkable amount of time finding his clods of turf and stomping them back from whence they came.

**div·ot, n.** a piece of turf gouged out with a club in making a stroke ; see CLOD.

**clod, n.** 1. a lump of earth or clay. 2. adj. a very stupid person ; see dolt

**dolt, n.** a dull stupid person ; a blockhead.

THE DOLT

THE DIVOT

# DRINKING AND EATING

These two interrelated activities not only take place before and after a round of golf, but, thanks to the existence of a "drink shack" on the 10th tee, they also occur *during* the round.

Time is exhausted not only in the mere ordering and consuming of food and drink, but also in the odd tradition of rolling dice to determine who will pick up the tab.

The act of rolling the dice among several people proves quite time-consuming, as does the verbal abuse and occasional fisticuffs resulting from accusations of cheating during the roll-off.

THE OLD TRADITION OF DICE ROLLING FOR THE BAR TAB

# GOLF CART ANTICS

*Golf cart antics* refers to a diverse group of activities having absolutely nothing to do with the game of golf itself that are performed with the aid of a motorized golf cart.

Typically, these activities take the form of little games that begin shortly after everyone's golf game has gone tohellinahandbasket, thus extinguishing any desire to continue playing the game of golf.

## *JOUSTING*

As in the medieval days, this game involves two mounted contestants squaring off against one another with lance in hand.

Separated by a distance of some 50 yards, the two contestants accelerate toward one another with the intention of uncarting the opponent.

The weapon d'uncarting is always the 1-wood, which is held parallel to the ground with the bulbous head aimed at one's opponent and the club grip firmly tucked under the armpit.

In the event that one of the contestants breaks or loses his lance on the first pass, it is customary for both contestants to draw their

GOLF CART ANTICS: THE JOUST

pitching wedge and use it in hatchet-like fashion on the second pass.

The game ends when one of the contestants is knocked from his cart or when both contestants run out of clubs.

## JUMP THE CREEK

A very simple game, really, yet one that requires a certain amount of intestinal fortitude, *Jump the Creek* involves crossing over a body of water without the aid of a bridge.

Gasoline-powered carts have a distinct advantage over electric carts because they generally possess a greater capacity for speed and acceleration than their electric counterparts.

## POLO

Like the game played on horseback, this version of polo involves opposing teams attempting to strike a single golf ball the length of a fairway and into the hole on the green while riding in a golf cart.

The putter is usually selected for use as a mallet because its short length makes it more easily wielded than the other clubs in one's golf bag.

Most golf courses frown on this activity due to the damaging effect that errant swings of the putter and spinning golf cart tires have on golf course greens.

## GOLF CART ANTICS : JUMP THE CREEK

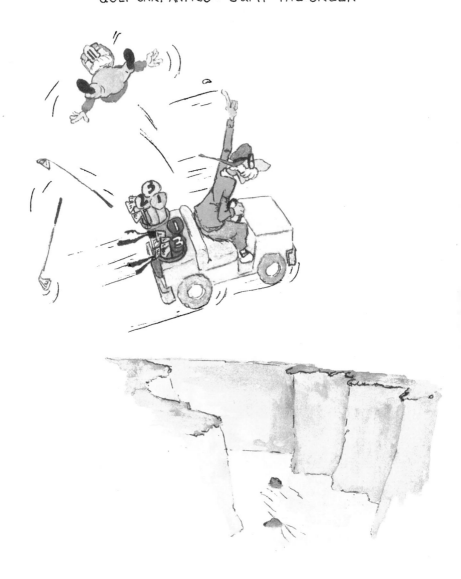

# LBAPBs

Nobody, but nobody, enjoys the task of searching for another golfer's lost golf ball, even if the lost ball belongs to one's teammate.

Still, it is in particularly poor taste to ignore a lost ball all points bulletin (LBAPB) issued by a fellow golfer, so one should always go through the motions of earnestly helping in the search.

The scenario resulting from said **LBAPB** is three or four golfers trudging through field, forest, and stream with all but one of the golfers muttering obscenities under their breath.

It should also be noted that it is very rude for an individual to issue more than two or three LBAPBs per round of golf, and in doing so one may well jeopardize one's chances of ever being asked to play the game of golf again.

I'M GLAD WE FOUND YOUR BALL, CHARLES.
NOW ALL WE HAVE TO DO IS FIND OUT WHERE
THE HELL <u>WE</u> ARE!

# MULLIGANS

It has been statistically proven that 99 percent of the shots taken from the first tee go awry.

More specifically, after being struck the ball will take a sudden left (hook) or right (slice) turn in midair, or will blaze a trail into the tall grass located a few feet in front of the tee, or in the most extreme cases will remain exactly in place (aka a swing and a miss).

This phenomenon occurs primarily because golfers panic at the mere thought of having to hit their first shot of the day in full view of their fellow golfers gathered in the pro shop, clubhouse, and practice area.

As a concession to the devastating effect this problem has on golfers it has become customary to allow for the hitting of two drives from the first tee. One may then select the better of the two shots without taking a penalty stroke.

This activity is known as taking a *Mulligan* and, although completely illegal, it has become an acceptable activity due to its common use on the course.

Another form of Mulligan is the *Roving Mulligan*, whereby one may save his Mulligan for use on any of the 18 tees.

One can easily understand the massive amount of time consumed by this activity since it multiplies everything from practice swings to divot replacement by two.

# PRACTICING

Not only does this activity incorporate the 300 or so practice swings taken during a round of golf, but it also includes the hitting of golf balls on the practice range and the chipping and putting of golf balls near and on the practice green.

It is not unusual, then, for practicing to consume as much as 25 percent of one's time spent on and about the golf course.

But, you may say, doesn't such practice involve the *striking* of golf balls? Yes, but whacking at the ball on the practice range and green *is* included as a non-golf-ball-striking activity, despite the apparent contradiction.

The rationale behind this classification is as follows:

1. Strokes taken in the practice area are not recorded, nor included in one's score.
2. Poor shots taken in the practice area may be casually explained away by such offhanded remarks as "I'm just experimenting with a new swing (stance, grip, club, etc.)."
3. As a result of 1 or 2 above, even the poorest of practice shots are unlikely to affect one's image as a golfer.

# RELOADING

In the (very likely) event that one manages to stroke one's golf ball out of bounds, one is then assessed a 1-stroke penalty and given the distinct privilege of hitting a second golf ball from the very same spot.

This charming little ritual is commonly referred to as *reloading* and is identical in format to a Mulligan except for the assessment of the penalty stroke.

Quite frankly, it is one of the most dreaded activities to occur on the golf course and a prime instigator of caddy harassment.

TEED OFF

RETEED

GOLF TEE

TEE BOX

MR. FARNSWORTH WAS QUITE TEED OFF THAT HIS INITIAL TEE OFF WENT OUT OF BOUNDS, WHICH MEANT HE HAD TO RETEE HIS BALL ON THE TEE IN THE TEE BOX SO HE COULD AGAIN TEE OFF.

# Score Keeping

This activity simply entails the penciling in of each player's score in a given box on the scorecard. Not too time-consuming one would think.

Wrong. As we have already noted, golfers tend to cheat. As a result one has to keep track not only of one's own score, but that of his opponent as well.

Invariably, one golfer will catch another golfer cheating and will diplomatically point out the error in addition. While diplomacy usually resolves the matter peaceably, arguments do sometimes erupt (see "Cheating" in Chapter 3).

# SETTLING UP

This activity usually takes place at the end of a round of golf and refers to the calculation and collection of money owed one golfer by another.

Now, there are essentially three stages to settling up, all of which can produce heated arguments fueled by the alcoholic beverages over which such computations are done.

The first stage involves trying to remember the rules, handicaps, and wagered amounts that were established on the first tee.

The second stage involves determining the actual dollar amount owed to and by the various golfers in the group.

The third and final stage involves owees getting the owers to pay up.

In addition to being snoopy, competitive little cheats, golfers are also known to be cheap little buggers. So it is not at all unusual for fisticuffs, or at the very least verbal abuse, to erupt over a $2 or $3 debt.

BY HEAVENS, GEORGIE, I REALLY DO OWE YOU $32,000!

# TANTRUMS

Although a great deal of verbal abuse, general harassment, and even fisticuffs occurs among golfers on the golf course, the term *tantrum* refers specifically to the activity of *self*-abuse, which is generated solely by an indivdual's pathetic performance on the golf course.

Tantrums can range from the mundane insulting of oneself to the more entertaining self-inflicted wound, such as whacking oneself in the shin with one's putter after missing an eight-inch putt for a birdie.

The typical tantrum scenario involves firmly grasping the end of the club with which one has just hit a particularly pathetic shot and with the aid of one or two pirouettes launching that club skyward.

Much time is spent not only in performing the tantrum, but also in retrieving the launched club, which almost certainly has traveled a good bit farther than the poorly hit golf ball.

# TRAP RAKING

Located sporadically about most holes on a golf course are large ditches filled with sand, which are known as *bunkers* or *sand traps*.

Commonly referred to as *the beach* by those familiar with the game, a bunker is a remarkably difficult spot from which to hit a golf ball.

The most time-consuming activity associated with bunkers is trap raking, whereby a golfer smooths out all the footprints and divots he made in the sand while attempting to dislodge his ball.

One positive aspect of trap raking is that it often proves excellent therapy (just like cutting out little paper dolls) in tranquilizing the irate golfer who has just spent three or four strokes in freeing his ball from the bunker.

TRAP RAKING OFTEN PROVES EXCELLENT THERAPY

# II.

# HOW TO LOOK GOOD WHEN YOU'RE NOT

# CHAPTER PRETEST

Take a few moments to carefully consider the two fellows pictured at right. One of these fellows goes by the rather cumbersome name of Winfield Southgate Westminster Farnsworth III and the other fellow by the name of Marvin Blit.

Additionally, one of these fellows is a pretty good amateur golfer, who regularly scores in the 80s, while the other fellow is a relatively poor amateur golfer, regularly scoring well in excess of 100.

Having finished your examination of the two golfers, answer the following questions.

Question 1: Which of these fellows (figure **A** or **B**) is our Mr. Winfield Southgate Westminster Farnsworth III?
Figure ___

Question 2: Which of the fellows (figure **A** or **B**) is the good amateur golfer, regularly scoring in the 80s?
Figure ___

figure **A.**          figure **B.**

It should not come as a surprise that our Mr. Farnsworth is the fellow found in figure **B**. One only has to consider those muttonchop sideburns and the indignant "harumphing" to reach the logical and correct conclusion.

If doubt remains, however, one might meditate on the gentleman's attire. Either the man's tailor is an ex–Good Humor Man or the man comes from a background where dressing like a box of Crayola crayons is not only acceptable, but considered chic.

With regard to the second question, if you selected figure **A** as the good amateur golfer, you are correct. In doing so, however, you have revealed that either (a) you have a markedly low IQ or (b) you're a bloody cheater.

In the latter case it can be said that your penchant for cheating indicates a remarkable aptitude for the game of golf, and you will find Chapter 3 particularly intriguing.

In the former case it can be said that one's IQ level has no bearing on the quality of one's golf game, so not to worry.

The more intelligent and honest of you selected figure B as the good amateur golfer. The fact that you were in error is of little consequence, but what is of consequence is *why* you made the incorrect assumption.

Without the benefit of seeing Messrs. Farnsworth and Blit whacking about a golf ball, you were forced to make your assumpiton based only on appearance.

You assumed that our Mr. Farnsworth, resplendent in fluorescent wardrobe and vast array of golf weaponry, had to be the fellow who regularly scores in the 80s. Adorning oneself in a manner and fashion similar to our Mr. Farnsworth, you too can convince the golfing public that you're one pretty good golfer . . . even when you're not.

# Golf Clubs: Weaponry Of The Game

The first thing one should understand about golf clubs is that golfers never call them *golf clubs*. Instead, golfers have developed such diverse nomenclature as *clubs, sticks, blades,* and *tallywackers* with which to refer to their golf clubs.

*Golf club* is actually a genus name for three distinct species of weaponry known as *woods, irons,* and *putters*.

Not unlike their would-be master, the amateur golfer, members of the wood species are noted for their bulbous, blocklike, and (usually) wooden head. This massive head and the great length of the club shaft make the wood species best suited for the longest and (usually) most embarrassing of golf shots.

The iron species is a far more diverse group than the larger wood species, ranging in size from the long and elegant 1-iron to the short and squatty sand wedge. Their hatchet-like club head and moderate shaft length make members of the iron species most aerodynamically appropriate for club-toss tantrums.

Finally, there is the gnome-like putter species, whose members are so short in stature as to be barely perceptible within the cavernous confines of a golf bag. Although these cute little buggers are predominantly used on and around the putting green, they have more recently gained popularity as cart polo mallets due to their light and wieldy nature.

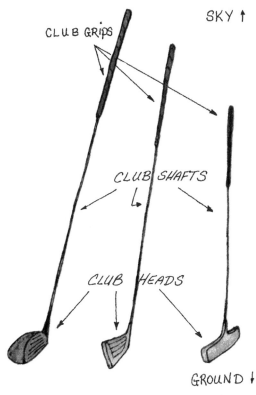

CLUB GRIPS

SKY ↑

CLUB SHAFTS

CLUB HEADS

GROUND ↓

WOODS    IRONS    PUTTERS

One should clearly understand that the proper assemblage of the golf club genus is critical to establishing one's image as a competent golfer— so much so that one should be gravely concerned about the proper representation of each species in one's golf bag.

Several schools of thought have emerged over the past three decades as to how best to go about selecting one's assemblage of golf clubs, the most prominent of which are outlined on the following pages.

### THE E-FLAT BAG SLAM RULE

This methodology sprang from the 1947 efforts of one L. D. Arnold to prove her theory that the golf bag was a viable form of musical instrument.

A music appreciation major at Duke University, Ms. Arnold locked herself in the chapel bell tower with no less than 147 golf bags containing varying assemblages of golf clubs.

She attempted to play John Philip Sousa's *Stars and Stripes Forever* by lobbing golf bags of different pitch from the bell tower, but the project came to an end when Ms. Arnold forgot to let go of the 117th golf bag.

What Ms. Arnold did determine prior to her rather abrupt departure from the bell tower was that a properly filled (with golf clubs) golf bag consistently generated an E-flat when thrown to the ground from a height of over two stories.

Of course this led to golfing novices everywhere lobbing their golf bags from tall buildings in an effort to achieve the now famous E-flat and thereby the perfect assemblage of golf clubs.

With the introduction of new materials such as aluminum and graphite into the construction of golf clubs, the E-flat Bag Slam Rule died a natural death, which is more than can be said for Ms. Arnold.

DUKE UNIVERSITY
DURHAM, NORTH CAROLINA

## *The FPF Silhouette Rule*

Developed in 1962 by one F. P. Frefre, this methodology dictates that one continue to stuff golf clubs of varying shapes and sizes into one's golf bag until the arrangement of clubs protruding from the bag closely resembles the silhouette of the New York City skyline.

The major problem with the FPF Silhouette Rule was that it didn't pass the Nosy Inspection of Your Golf Bag Test. This occurs when one of your snoopy golfing compatriots walks up and blatantly begins to inspect the contents of your golf bag!

NYC SKYLINE                    GOLF CLUB PROFILE

No matter how great the silhouette of your golf bag looks at a distance, it is distinctly possible under the FPF Silhouette Rule to omit several important clubs or, worse yet, end up with several of the same club, such as four of the 3-iron.

If this catastrophe strikes, you will end up looking quite silly because anyone who has actually played the game knows that one *never* carries more than one of any size golf club, with the possible exception of an extra putter or driver with which one is experimenting.

## THE "THE CLOSER THEY GET, THE BETTER YOU LOOK" RULE

Devised in 1973 by two undergraduate accounting majors at Loyola (New Orleans) University, this methodology is a bit more complex than its predecessors in that it requires one to have the ability to read and count to 14.

According to the United States Golf Association, the maximum number of golf clubs one may carry about during a match is 14. Since virtually all golf bag snoops have memorized the USGA Rule Book, or at the very least carry it around in their back pocket, they are very much aware of this trivia tidbit. It is imperative, then, that one . . .

### a. Never Carry More than 14 Golf Clubs.

As noted in our discussion of the FPF Silhouette Rule, the carrying of more than one of any particular club indicates a complete lack of familiarity with the game and will blow one's cover as a competent golfer. Alarmed by the increasing frequency of such embarrassing episodes, golf club manufacturers began numbering the various golf club sizes, and golfers should utilize these little numbers to ensure that they . . .

## DON'T DUPLICATE

### b. Never Carry More than One of Any Particular Club.

Because of their great length and bulbous club head, including several members of the wood species in one's golf bag will greatly enhance the distant profile of one's golf club collection.

Additionally, one should specifically include the 1-wood, aka *driver* only because it is bloody well impossible to use in properly hitting a golf ball. The mere presence of this beast in one's golf bag will effectively stifle many golf bag snoops by implying that the bearer is one of the elite few capable of effectively using the bloody thing! So . . .

### c. Always Carry a Minimum of Three Woods, Including the 1-wood, aka Driver.

Consulting the previously mentioned little numbers on the bottom of the golf club, one will notice that irons are numbered 1 through 10 and vary greatly in both size and shape. While consensus of opinion dictates that one include a minimum of four irons in one's golf bag, the question remains as to which four clubs to select.

Disregarding the seldom-used 1-iron and 10-iron as mere collector's items, one should select all the even (or odd) numbered clubs from the remaining 2- through 9-irons to insure as diverse a collection as possible. The operative rule here is to . . .

### d. Always Carry a Minimum of Four Even (or Odd) Numbered Irons.

The putter species and the wedge members of the iron species are so short in stature that they add very little to the distant profile of one's club collection, yet they are absolutely critical in passing an up-close and personal inspection. Therefore, one should . . .

IN RESPONSE TO MR. DINSMORE'S DISCOVERY OF TOO MANY GOLF CLUBS IN HIS BAG, MR. WINSLOW REMEDIED THE PROBLEM IN THE MOST APPROPRIATE MANNER!

### e. Always Carry a Putter, Sand Wedge, and Pitching Wedge.

Our paradigm golf bag now contains three woods, four irons, a putter, a sand wedge, and a pitching wedge. Those who can't add up the total again exhibit low IQs and high potential as golfers. Others, however, will instantly realize that . . .

## f. The Minimum Number of Golf Clubs One Should Carry is 10.

There are several options open to the amateur golfer in filling the void between the minimum (10) and maximum (14) number of clubs one should carry about the course, all of which will greatly enhance one's image as a competent golfer:

**Extra Putter and/or Driver**: Representing the lone exceptions to the "Don't Duplicate" rule, the inclusion of an extra putter or driver will convince the golf bag snoop that one has mastered the game of golf and is now just tinkering with its finer points.

**1-Iron and/or 10-Iron**: In addition to being wonderful collector's items, having these clubs in one's collection may well convince the golf bag snoop that one is the lone amateur golfer capable of hitting a golf ball (somewhere) with them.

**Baffler**: Recently introduced by golf club manufacturers, this newest addition to the wood species is the rage of golf club fashion. Who cares how to use it?

**Add Odds to Evens**: One might prefer simply to add the odd numbered irons (3, 5, 7, and 9) to the four even numbered irons (2, 4, 6, and 8) one initially selected—a boring but nevertheless functional option.

PROFILE PERSPECTIVE

AERIAL (SNOOP) PERSPECTIVE

# GOLF BAG: THE NOUN

On occasion and with a *remarkable* amount of discretion, the term *golf bag* is used in reference to a golfer's spouse, but it is more widely and safely used in reference to the peculiar-looking object at right.

The primary function of this object, which closely resembles an overgrown wastebasket with pockets, is to hold one's golf equipment.

From a functional perspective it might be argued that there is little difference from one golf bag to the next, but this rather myopic perspective would also argue that there is little difference between a rowboat and a yacht.

Consider again Messrs. Blit and Farnsworth, depicted at the beginning of this chapter, and in particular their respective golf bags. Certainly this piece of golf equipment is a relevant factor in the total image presented by each of these fellows.

Out of the vast spectrum of potential golf bag acquisitions, then, what guidelines might we offer to aid the golfer in his selection?

Detailed study of the golf bag as an image factor has only recently begun, so a precise methodology for proper golf bag selection has not yet emerged. Still, a certain consensus of opinion has been reached regarding three rules of thumb:

### 1. Bulky is Beautiful.

Apparently, "the bigger the golf bag, the better the image" is the philosophy currently in vogue.

### 2. Gadgets are Gorgeous.

Gadgets are a superb addition to one's golf bag, particularly electronic ones. Portable telephones, TVs, and wet bars markedly improve the quality of one's golf bag and thereby the image of the golfer. Bear in mind, however, that the golf bag itself is the key element. A shag-bag equipped with a porta-phone is not as good for one's image as a big and bulky bag without a porta-phone.

### 3. There's Always a Bulk and Buck Compromise.

Even when armed according to the above two guidelines, chances are that price will be the deciding factor in one's golf bag selection.

One should be sure in budgeting for the acquisition of a golf bag to set aside some funds for the caddy and/or golf cart fees. The last thing one will want to do is spend every last cent on the biggest and bulkiest of golf bags and then have to haul the bloody thing around on one's own shoulder!

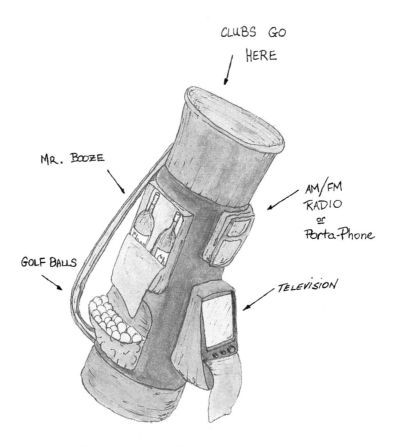

CLUBS GO
HERE

MR. BOOZE

AM/FM
RADIO
or
Porta-Phone

GOLF BALLS

TELEVISION

## THE GOLF BAG

# GOLF BALLS: THE AWOL AMMO

As in the case of golf clubs, there are pages upon pages in the USGA Rule Book that dictate what constitutes a legal golf ball. Completely ignore such trivia!

Any golf ball purchased from a conventional sporting goods store or pro shop will meet the USGA regulations, leaving one to concentrate on the more subtle aspects of golf ball selection.

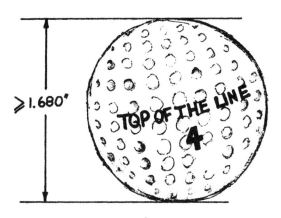

$\geqslant 1.680''$

weight $\leqslant 1.620$ ounces

## COLOR CODE

Not too long ago all golf balls were white, but now the little creatures are available in a spectrum of colors rivaling a rainbow.

Many golfers mistakenly select a fluorescent red, yellow, orange, or green golf ball based on the assumption that they will be more easily located on the course, but the fact of the matter is that it's just as difficult to find one of the fluorescent variety as a standard white ball when it's lying in 6 inches of grass or 10 feet of water.

In light of this fact, the sole guideline one should utilize in selecting the color of one's golf ball is to make sure that it doesn't clash with one's wardrobe. Given the rather unusual attire many golfers don for an outing of golf, this is not as easy a task as it may first appear.

### *Old Ball/New Ball Economy Exchange*

At a mere cost of $1.50 to $2.00 each for top-of-the-line golf balls, most golfing novices make the mistake of considering the little buggers an inexpensive commodity.

It takes only a few rounds of golf, however, for the golfing rookie to come to the startling conclusion that *golf balls have a nasty and consistent habit of permanently disappearing from sight.* More specifically, it is not at all unusual to lose well over 100 of the creatures during a golf season, with the result that golf ball purchases may well represent over a $200 nondeductible expense.

A methodology was developed in 1967 by Mr. M. D. Hannibal to dramatically reduce golf ball costs without compromising one's image as a golfer.

1. On the first tee one should pull out a shiny, new, top-of-the-line golf ball and leisurely toss it around for a bit until everyone notices its fine quality.
2. After completing the first hole one should put the (hopefully still) shiny and new golf ball back in one's golf bag and pull out a "used" ball for use on the next 16 holes. "Used" balls are dingy and scuffed up at the least and often have little smiles on their faces because they are so happy to be pulled out of retirement.
3. On the 18th tee, one should reverse the exchange so as to finish the round of golf with an impressive-looking golf ball in the event that one might be noticed upon coming into view of the clubhouse again.

"Used" golf balls are typically not available from the same retail outlets one would seek out to procure top-of-the-line golf balls. Instead, they are accumulated on a minimal cost basis from local garage sales, or they are stolen from practice areas on an altogether-no-charge basis.

The most popular brand of "used" golf balls is apparently manufactured by the RANGE Company and is readily identifiable by the thick red stripe around its circumference.

# CARTS VERSUS CADDIES

The quality of one's golf game will ultimately dictate whether one should use a golf cart or a caddy as a toter of one's golf equipment.

The advantages peculiar to both the golf cart and caddy are outlined on pages 86 and 87, and in carefully reviewing this presentation one will come to realize that virtually all of the advantages associated with using a caddy stem from the humanoid nature of the beast.

Unlike the golf cart, the caddy comes equipped with a brain, making him capable of speech, sight, and autonomous locomotion.

Additionally, the caddy is equipped with a finely tuned central nervous system, which makes the little fellows remarkably responsive to beratement, torture, and general harassment.

Note, however, that the very human characteristics that can make the caddy so functionally advantageous also make the caddy a potentially deadly adversary. One should clearly understand that many caddies are blabbermouths. They not only are capable of, but actually enjoy, ratting on a golfer.

With this in mind, it is strongly recommended that only good golfers use caddies. As a poor golfer one must forgo the pleasures of caddy harassment and absorb the higher costs of renting a golf cart in order to protect one's image as a good golfer.

Poor golfers, then, should always use golf carts. In addition to being inanimate objects, and therefore incapable of ratting on golfers, golf carts have other advantages that help to compensate for the pleasure derived from caddy harassment that is lost.

The greater load capacity of the golf cart enables one to carry about such luxury items as television sets and beer coolers, which can prove very pleasant distractions from one's pathetic attempts to play golf.

After one's game has deteriorated to a point where even a cold brew and a good soap opera are not enough of a distraction, one might then use the golf cart to play other games (see "Golf Cart Antics").

THE ONLY THING A CADDY ENJOYS MORE THAN RATTING
ON A GOLFER IS THE EXTORTION OF
MONEY FROM SAID GOLFER.

# CARTS VERSUS CADDIES

| Features | Golf Carts | Caddies |
|---|---|---|
| 1. Capable of tracking, finding, and retrieving errant shots of the golf ball.<br>2. Capable of offering worthwhile advice on such subjects as wind direction, distance of shot, and club selection. | Typically the golf cart is incapable of assisting in areas 1 and 2. Note, however, that some privately owned golf carts with sonar/radar and computerized club selection programming are vastly superior to the caddy in these areas. | Although the caddy is capable of assisting in areas 1 and 2, very few of the little buggers perform the tasks very effectively, if at all. Thus, while the caddy should hold a distinct advantage over the golf cart in these areas, often the advantage is negligible. |
| 3. Capable of responding satisfactorily to verbal abuse, torture, and harassment. | As inanimate objects, golf carts are incapable of responding to punishment, so they are virtually no fun to harass. | Capable of fear, pain, and gut-wrenching screams, the caddy is far more satisfying to punish than a golf cart. |
| 4. Capable of turning one in for cheating.<br>5. Capable of blatantly laughing in one's face over one's pathetic endeavors.<br>6. Capable of revealing the true caliber of one's golf | As inanimate objects, golf carts are incapable of making fun of a golfer. They are equally incapable of revealing the caliber of one's golf game or turning one in for cheating. | Not only are caddies capable of ratting on and razzing their clients, but they will go to great lengths to put a golfer through the wringer. |

| | Golf Cart | Caddy |
|---|---|---|
| game to each and every person in the vicinity of the golf course. | | Caddies are slow. Caddies have the temperament of a mule. Caddies sweat. Caddies will not carry anything more than a golf bag. Caddies make lousy bartenders. |
| 7. Capable of maintaining land speeds in excess of 5 mph and carrying a load in excess of 150 pounds over the 18 holes of the golf course. | The golf cart is capable of much greater speeds than the caddy as well as considerably larger payloads; e.g., coolers, wet bars, and TVs. Its speed and load capacity allows for usage in games other than golf (see "Golf Cart Antics"). | |
| 8. Available at reasonable rates. | Golf carts are expensive to rent at $20 to $30 for 18 holes. | Caddies are inexpensive relative to the golf cart. If the golf cart goes for $25, the caddy will go for $15 plus tip. |
| 9. Available for ownership. | Though outrageously expensive, the outright ownership of a golf cart is totally chic. In terms of a single acquisition, the purchase of a golf cart is the crème de la creme of image enhancers. | The Civil Rights Act of 1968 clearly and finally outlawed the ownership of caddies. |

# WARDROBE: MY NAME IS NOT BOZO, NOR AM I BY PROFESSION A CLOWN

The final step in equipping oneself for the game of golf, and at the same time maximizing one's image as a competent golfer, is wardrobe selection. In reviewing the two-step apparel acquisition methodology outlined below, one will come to understand that a golfer's taste in fashion might more precisely be referred to as a taste for the absurd.

1. The golfer should assemble an outfit that makes him look as silly as possible.
2. The golfer should always select bright and fluorescent colors so that he clashes with any and all conceivable surroundings. Good choices are raucous red, outrageous orange, and shimmering chartreuse.

# III.

# FAILING ALL ELSE, CHEAT!

Despite incessant warnings against the activity, amateur golfers invariably make the rather momentous mistake of endeavoring to play a round of golf in full view of the general golfing public.

While it is true that some amateur golfers are unwittingly or unwillingly duped, badgered, or coerced into playing a round of golf, an incredible 97 percent of the dummies actually report to the first tee on a *voluntary* basis!

This is a dumbfounding statistic in light of the fact that the undertaking will result in the complete destruction of the golfing novice's carefully and expensively groomed facade as a competent golfer.

The reason for this illogical behavior apparently stems from the amateur golfer's nasty habit of falling prey to the very illusion so painstakingly created. Caught up in the splendor of his dazzling new golfing wardrobe and weaponry, the golfing rookie comes to the utterly absurd conclusion that he can actually play the bloody game!

Typically, the catastrophic reality of the situation does not dawn upon the amateur golfer until he is standing on the first tee with club in hand, the match just moments from getting under way.

IF YOU DON'T CHEAT YOU'RE
ONLY CHEATING YOURSELF!

Far too committed to withdraw from the golf game, how might one avoid the seemingly inevitable destruction of one's image as a competent golfer?

*One cheats.*

Bear in mind, too, that we are not talking about the wimpy "here a stroke, there a stroke" forms of cheating.

No, we're talking about "magnitude cheating." More specifically, cheating with imagination and a frequency that can shave 70 to 80 strokes off one's final score.

Cheating techniques are born of one's imagination in illegally resolving what are otherwise legally unresolvable golfing predicaments. Therefore, the number and variety of cheating techniques available to the amateur golfer are bounded only by the fertility of one's imagination.

Still, certain golfing predicaments, and the cheating techniques used to resolve them, apparently recur with enough frequency as to be worthy of special note.

Initially, it should be pointed out that cheating techniques fall into one of two general categories known as *open-field cheating* and *covert cheating*. The former category refers to cheating techniques performed in full view of one's golfing compatriots, while the latter category refers to techniques that might be used while hidden from view.

DISTRACTION IS THE KEY
TO SUCCESSFUL CHEATING.

# OPEN-FIELD CHEATING

Since it is of paramount importance that one does not get caught cheating for fear of bodily injury and social ostracism, it is imperative that one's open-field cheating techniques be markedly subtle in nature and finely honed with frequent practice.

In point of fact, time is more productively spent rehearsing one's cheating techniques than attempting to master the proper method of swatting a bloody golf ball.

## *KEEPING OF THE SCORE*

In order to fully comprehend the simplicity and productivity of the cheating techniques that fall into this category, let us first consider what transpires during the scorekeeping process:

Step 1. Upon the completion of any given hole a golfer is expected to add up each and every stroke attempted in (eventually) getting his golf ball from the tee into the cup.

Step 2. The golfer then reports this score to the keeper of the scorecard.

Step 3. The scorekeeper tallies the reported score on the scorecard.

BY MEANS OF A SIMPLE PREVARICATION
AFTER EACH AND EVERY HOLE ONE
MIGHT EASILY SHAVE SOME 20 TO 30
STROKES OFF ONE'S FINAL SCORE.

Clearly, this process just *oozes* cheat potential!

Consider, for example, the productive effect of a simple prevarication at step 2. One might readily shave some 20 to 30 strokes off one's actual final score by simply lying to the scorekeeper after each and every hole.

Always remember, however, that subtlety is the key to any successful cheating endeavor, as evidenced in the following presentation of the more respected cheating techniques associated with scorekeeping.

### Bibbity, Bobbity, Boo.

Introduced in 1907 by perhaps the most famous of golf course prevaricators, Mr. Francis "Magic" Patrick, this technique involves bedazzling one's fellow golfers with both word and gesture as outlined below.

- Never report your score until the scorekeeper asks for it, but determine ahead of time what score you would like to receive.
- When the scorekeeper requests your score, offer up your prevarication and wait for his eyes to start bugging out of his head.

- Using the scorekeeper's bug-eyed/red-faced countenance as a cue, make a grandiose turn away from the scorekeeper (so he won't see you giggling) and gaze back upon the hole just played.
- With one hand shading your brow, begin pointing at specific spots on the golf course with your other hand, while offering up some detailed narrative, such as "Let's see now . . . I was under the tree in one . . . in the left rough in two . . .," etc.
- Put them (strokes) together and what do you get? Bibbity, bobbity, par (four)!

Rumored to have once explained away seven full strokes in recording a bibbity, bobbity, birdie (three) on the second hole at Kirtland Country Club, Mr. Magic offered the following commentary on his successful use of this technique shortly before his sentencing on a mail fraud conviction:

"Style and finesse are the foundation of any successful con job . . . by the time I finished my performance . . . I received a standing ovation . . . and an eagle one on a par three!"

## Take the Stroke Control.

Believe it or not, this one is actually legal!

So as not to inflate a golfer's handicap due to (supposedly) one or two particularly horrible holes, there is actually a limit as to the number of strokes one may record on any given hole.

A particularly poor golfer (as are all golfing novices) may not, for example, record anything higher than a triple bogey.

If this little rule does not appear to offer much relief, one might consider the not unlikely scenario of plunking four straight tee shots into the moat surrounding a quaint par three.

Teeing up for the ninth shot of the hole with the moat yet to be negotiated, not even Mr. Magic could bibbity, bobbity, bogey this hole, and a triple bogey six is an appetizing alternative!

Additionally, one might take heart in learning that a triple bogey on each of the 18 holes would result in a score of about 125, which is some 50 strokes lower than one probably would have scored.

So, when you've butchered a hole to the extent that it's time to cut your losses, simply pick up your ball (assuming you can find it) and remark to the scorekeeper: "I'm out of this hole! Better just give me the old triple."

BOWED AND BLOODIED, MR. ANDERSON SIGNALS THE OTHER MEMBERS OF HIS FOURSOME THAT HE IS PICKING UP, AND TAKING A STROKE CONTROL 6.

## Use the Tuckster Tally.

As impressed as one might well be with the effectiveness of both the bibbity, bobbity, boo and stroke control techniques, they pale in comparison to the far greater cheat potential that one might realize by gaining control of the scorecard.

Affectionately christened the "Tuckster Tally," this cheating technique was first introduced by one Lawrence "Tuckster" Garvin at a 1957 company golf outing during which Mr. Garvin effectively swindled the company president out of $135.

Not only does the "Tuckster Tally" methodology dictate how to take command of the scorecard; it also details the intricate maneuvers that might then be used to lower one's score substantially.

1. *One must get control of the scorecard!* While this can usually be accomplished by simply volunteering to act as scorekeeper, one will occasionally find that this privilege has already been claimed by another member of the group. Do not argue the point for fear of arousing suspicion! Instead, find an opportune time to "lose" the usurper's scorecard so that the duty will quite naturally be reassigned to you.
2. *One should always carry an eraser-equipped pencil.* Golf course managers have become all

too familiar with the Tuckster Tally, and under
the guise of cutting costs they now issue
stubby eraserless pencils so as to discourage
cheating.

3. *Never give yourself a winning score.* Golfers are by nature a particularly selfish lot, their only cares being (1) *their* score and (2) winning. Until such time as you beat them, your companions will be completely indifferent to and oblivious of your score.
4. *Be patient with your par.* From time to time one of your compatriots will become aware of your *actual* score on a given hole, which will force you to record the pathetic endeavor. *Don't panic!* Several holes after the incident your score will fade from everyone's memory, at which time your eraser-tipped pencil can redefine that atrocious nine to par four.

A word of caution regarding the Tuckster Tally: on rare occasions golfers have been known to become so enamored with their creative writing efforts that they actually forget to play the hole. This lacks a certain amount of necessary subtlety and should be altogether avoided.

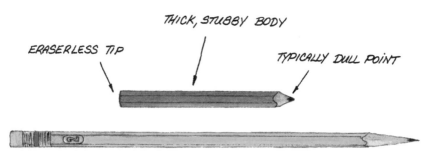

THICK, STUBBY BODY

ERASERLESS TIP

TYPICALLY DULL POINT

## CADDIEGATE

Amateur golfers often compound the enormity of their initial blunder (attempting to play the game) by contracting the services of a caddy.

As mentioned earlier, caddies can be particularly vicious beasts, and they are fully capable of enlightening the golfing community of one's forays into cheating.

The only way to extricate oneself from this unenviable position is to bribe the caddy.

The amount of the bribe to be offered is directly proportional to the frequency and severity of one's cheating activities on the golf course.

| NOT FOR PUBLICATION | | | |
|---|---|---|---|
| 1988 CHEAT & TIP SCHEDULE | | | |
| Cheat Scenario | Base Bribe × | Degree of Risk* | Bribe Tip |
| Lying about one's score | $1.00 | 17 | $17.00 |
| Pretending one found one's ball in the quicksand | $1.00 | 49 | $49.00 |
| Counting a swing and a miss as a practice swing | $1.00 | 2 | $ 2.00 |
| | | Total Bribe | $68.00 |

* Likelihood of someone believing the caddy if he turns you in (on a scale from 1 to 50, with 50 being most likely).

105

## CADDIEGATE II

For the golfing novice this cheat and tip routine is likely to get remarkably expensive due to the staggering amount of cheating required to save one's reputation, so one might give some serious thought to simply hiring the caddy as an aide de cheat.

The going rate for aides de cheat is $100 for nine holes, but some caddies offer season packages and special weekday rates.

Payment terms are typically cash in advance, under the table.

CADDIEGATE II

### *Heave, Lob And Kick Routines*

Heave, lob and kick techniques are designed to "improve" the position of one's golf ball by advancing it closer to the hole by some 3 feet to 60 yards, without the aid of a golf club or the assessment of a stroke.

While these techniques do not result in any direct stroke reduction, on a cumulative basis they might effectively shorten the course by some 600 to 900 yards.

On some very rare occasions (all of which should be seized) it is actually legal to pick up and move one's golf ball, but on no occasion may one move the golf ball closer to the hole. Therefore, one must distract one's golfing companions prior to advancing the ball.

Said distraction can usually be accomplished by means of a well-timed phrase such as "Pardon me, but isn't that your car being towed?"

Occasionally such simple distractions will be ignored, and less subtle endeavors must be undertaken, such as the old "Release the Golf Cart Emergency Brake" maneuver or the often used "Set Your Opponent's Golf Bag Afire" routine.

Distraction complete, one might then employ any of three ball advancement methods.

# THE KICK

**Try the Kick.**

Sometimes referred to as the "Pele Punt," this technique involves booting the golf ball with one's foot. The kick lacks a certain amount of accuracy and distance but is very well suited for dislodging the ball from behind tall trees or very thick rough.

### Use the Lob.

This maneuver is used primarily for midrange (5 to 15 yards) advancements that require some degree of accuracy.

Grasping the golf ball between thumb and forefinger, one tosses the ball toward the intended target in underhand fashion, not unlike the art of bowling.

This method is particularly productive on or about the putting green.

THE LOB

### Resort to the Heave.

Sometimes referred to as the "Lurching Launch" or the "Oaf Umph," this maneuver is used for the longest of illegal golf ball advancements.

The heave involves cradling the golf ball in the palm of one's hand and with the aid of a running start, flinging the ball forward in a manner similar to shot putting.

Unlike shot putting, however, one should *take care not to grunt* while releasing the golf ball for fear of drawing attention to one's cheating endeavor.

THE HEAVE

# COVERT CHEATING

Acts of covert cheating are intentionally carried out far from the scrutiny of one's golfing companions so that there is little likelihood of one's getting caught cheating. These endeavors therefore tend to be far more blatant than their open-field counterparts.

Naturally, one will be curious as to where best to conduct such covert activities.

While most accomplished golfers prefer to get from tee to green via the finely manicured carpet of grass known as the *fairway,* the covert cheater will find it far more intriguing to approach the green via the *foulway,* better known as *the rough.*

The very same deep grass and tall timber that comprise the foulway and strike fear in the hearts of competent golfers will offer the incompetent duffer some cozy camouflage under which to perform undetected acts of cheating.

At the very first opportunity, then, the golfing novice should *make every effort to swat the golf ball into the far reaches of the rough.*

Given the remarkable frequency with which this is accomplished on an unintentional basis by particularly good golfers, the *intentional* efforts of the golfing incompetent should meet with considerable success.

The foulway achieved, one might then initiate covert acts of cheating.

PLUNK!

COVERT (UNDERCOVER) CHEATING

From the almost unending array of covert cheating techniques two maneuvers deserve special mention, having gained particular notoriety and popularity among golfing cheats.

## THE POCKET PLOP

Although various semblances of the pocket plop technique have actually been in use since the turn of the 19th century, it was not until August 23, 1964, that the maneuver was formally quantified by one Melvin C. Arnbarn, while mulling over his record-setting performance of 44 lost golf balls over 18 holes of play.

A multimillionaire who insisted upon using nothing but top-of-the-line golf balls, Melvin was far less concerned with the $88 cost resulting from all those lost balls than with the assessment of the 44 penalty strokes to his final score.

After much consideration it finally dawned on Mr. Arnbarn that his concern need not be with finding his *own* errant golf ball, but with finding *any* golf ball, and in that regard a few well-placed holes in one's pants pockets would offer much assistance.

The following plop methodology eventually evolved from Mr. Arnbarn's initial brainstorm.

1. The successful pocket plop maneuver first requires that one (a) remove the front pocket linings from one's golf trousers prior to undertaking a round and (b) carry a "spare" golf ball in one's back (still lined) pocket.
2. In anticipation of one's intentionally errant shot becoming all too errant, and otherwise lost, one should remove the "spare" golf ball

POCKET PLOPS SHOULD NOT BE ATTEMPTED WHILE WEARING SHORTS

from one's back pocket upon entering the foulway.

3. When it becomes abundantly clear that one's original golf ball has in fact vanished, the

"spare" ball should be slipped into one's liningless front pocket and allowed to trickle down the inside of the pant leg.

4. Upon its safe arrival into the rough below, one might subtly substitute the "spare" ball for the now lost ball with the expression "Oh, here it is! Jeepers, the grass is so thick in here I almost stepped on it!"

**CAUTION: Do not attempt pocket plops while wearing shorts!**

Thanks in large part to the plop maneuver, Mr. Arnbarn has not suffered a single lost ball penalty stroke during the 20-plus years since his record-breaking performance.

It is interesting to note, however, that during the same time frame the range ball population at Mr. Arnbarn's golf club has decreased by some 6,317 golf balls.

## *Tee Time*

The odd little gadget illustrated below is known as a *golf tee*, and it serves the lone function on the golf course of elevating one's golf ball from the surrounding terrain so that one might take a more unobstructed whack at said golf ball and thereby hit it farther.

The lone area of the golf course where one might *legally* use a golf tee is on the tee box that initiates each of the 18 holes on the course, but

TEE TIME

legalities should be of little concern to a would-be golf cheat, and one will find the timely use of a tee or two considerably helpful in escaping the confines of the foulway.

The effectiveness of what has come to be called the "tee time" technique is borne out by the *almost* successful efforts of one Gregory C. Hausen during the 1933 Highland Country Club Championship.

A rather large fellow with a particularly vicious if not accurate golf swing, Mr. Hausen managed to launch his initial drive of the campaign some 300 yards forward of the tee box but some 75 yards right of the fairway.

Gazing down upon his pocket-plopped golf ball (the original proved quite lost), it occurred to Mr. Hausen that a crunching 3-wood would prove a far more productive method of ball advancement than the heave maneuver were it not for the fact that his ball was submerged in the thick underbrush of the foulway.

Necessity being the mother of invention, Mr. Hausen set his golf ball atop a discreetly placed golf tee and proceeded to smash the little bugger some 200 yards toward the green.

So taken was Mr. Hausen with the productivity of his initial tee time technique that he employed it no less than 27 times during the course of his match. Alas, his impressive performance went for naught as he failed to tip his caddy and was promptly turned in for his cheating endeavors.

# Epilogue

Having offered considerable instruction as to the proper manner to behave, dress, and equip oneself on and about a golf course, I think it appropriate to again caution the would-be golfer against ever taking up the sport.

Golf, you see, is not a game, but an addiction that draws unassuming clods like me deeper and deeper into its seductive web.

Like any worthwhile bad habit, the more one plays the game, the more one wants to play the game, and at four to five hours per round of golf severe marital distress can result from the addiction unless one's spouse has also been afflicted.

Financial ruin is a distinct possibility due to the expensive nature of the sport, and of course moral corruption is completely unavoidable thanks to the incessant temptations to gamble, curse, lie, and cheat.

The most terrifying aspect of the affliction, however, is that it can maim, and even kill! Hypertension, heart disease, stroke and temporary insanity are but a few possible by-products of one's continuous frustration over attempting to properly hit a bloody little golf ball.

In conclusion, then, I would suggest that the would-be golfer consider this last piece of advice first:

NEVER TAKE UP THE GAME OF GOLF.